Write

Two One Act Plays

by Woody Allen

SAMUEL FRENCH

FOUNDED 1830

SAMUELFRENCH.COM

ISBN   978-0-573-62630-2   Printed in U.S.A.   #25746

MUSIC USE NOTE

Licensees are solely responsible for obtaining formal written permission from copyright owners to use copyrighted music in the performance of this play and are strongly cautioned to do so. If no such permission is obtained by the licensee, then the licensee must use only original music that the licensee owns and controls. Licensees are solely responsible and liable for all music clearances and shall indemnify the copyright owners of the play and their licensing agent, Samuel French, Inc., against any costs, expenses, losses and liabilities arising from the use of music by licensees.

IMPORTANT BILLING AND CREDIT REQUIREMENTS

All producers of *WRITER'S BLOCK must* give credit to the Author of the Play in all programs distributed in connection with performances of the Play, and in all instances in which the title of the Play appears for the purposes of advertising, publicizing or otherwise exploiting the Play and/or a production. The name of the Author *must* appear on a separate line on which no other name appears, immediately following the title and *must* appear in size of type not less than fifty percent of the size of the title type.

presents

Writer's Block

written and directed by
WOODY ALLEN

with

Kate Blumberg	**Heather Burns**	**Clea Lewis**
Bebe Neuwirth	**Richard Portnow**	**Paul Reiser**
Grant Shaud	**Skipp Sudduth**	**Jay Thomas**

Christopher Evan Welch

sets	*costumes*	*lighting*
Santo Loquasto	**Laura Bauer**	**James F. Ingalls**

sound	*casting*	*casting consultant*
Scott Myers	**Bernard Telsey Casting/ Will Cantler**	**Juliet Taylor**

production stage manager	*production manager*	*general manager*
Janet Takami	**Kurt Gardner**	**Ryan Freeman**

press representative
Boneau/Bryan-Brown

This production is presented in association with Letty Aronson.

CAST
(in order of appearance)

RIVERSIDE DRIVE

Jim	PAUL REISER
Fred	SKIPP SUDDUTH
Barbara	KATE BLUMBERG

Time/Place:
Midafternoon

OLD SAYBROOK

Sheila	BEBE NEUWIRTH
Norman	JAY THOMAS
Jenny	HEATHER BURNS
David	GRANT SHAUD
Hal	CHRISTOPHER EVAN WELCH
Sandy	CLEA LEWIS
Max	RICHARD PORTNOW

Time/Place:
Old Saybrook, Connecticut
Sunday afternoon

Assistant Stage Manager - Bethany Russell

CONTENTS

*Curtain rises on a gray day in New York. There might even be some
hint of fog. The setting suggests a secluded spot by the
embankment of the Hudson River where one can lean over the
rail, watch the boats and see the New Jersey shoreline.
Probably the West Seventies or Eighties.*

*JIM SWAIN, a writer, somewhere between forty and fifty, is waiting
nervously, checking his watch, pacing, trying a number on his
cellular phone to no response. He's obviously waiting to meet
someone.*

*He rubs his hands together, checks for some drizzle and perhaps
pulls his jacket up a bit as he feels at least a damp mist.*

*Presently, a large, homeless man, unshaven, a street dweller of
approximately JIM'S age, drifts on with a kind of eye on JIM.
His name is FRED.*

*FRED eventually drifts closer to JIM, who has become increasing-
ly aware of his presence and, while not exactly afraid, is wary
of being in a desolate area with a large, unsavory type. Add to
this that JIM wants his rendezvous with whomever he is waiting for to be very private. Finally, FRED engages him.*

FRED. Rainy day. *(JIM nods, agreeing but not wanting to
encourage conversation.)* A drizzle. *(JIM nods with a wan smile.)*
Or should I say mizzle—mist and drizzle.

JIM. Um.

FRED. *(Pause)* Look at how fast the current's moving. You throw your cap into the river it'll be out in the open sea in twenty minutes.

JIM. *(Begrudging but polite.)* Uh-huh . . .

FRED. *(Pause)* The Hudson River travels three hundred and fifteen miles beginning in the Adirondacks and emptying finally into the vast Atlantic Ocean.

JIM. Interesting.

FRED. No it's not. Ever wonder what it'd be like if the current ran in the opposite direction?

JIM. I haven't actually.

FRED. Chaos-the world would be out of sync. You throw your cap in it'd get carried up to Poughkeepsie rather than out to sea.

JIM. Yes . . . well . . .

FRED. Ever been to Poughkeepsie?

JIM. What?

FRED. Ever been to Poughkeepsie?

JIM. Me?

FRED. *(Looks around; they're alone.)* Who else?

JIM. Why do you ask?

FRED. It's a simple question.

JIM. If I was in Poughkeepsie?

FRED. Were you?

JIM. *(Considers the question, decides he'll answer.)* No, I haven't. OK?

FRED. So if you haven't, why are you so guilty?

JIM. Look, I'm a little preoccupied.

FRED. You don't come here often, do you?

JIM. Why?

FRED. Interesting.

JIM. What do you want? Are you going to hit me up for a touch? Here, here's a buck.

FRED. Hey—I only asked if you came here often.

JIM. *(Getting impatient.)* No. I'm meeting someone. I have a lot on my mind.

FRED. What a day you picked.

JIM. I didn't know it would be this nasty.

FRED. Don't you watch the weather on TV? Christ, it seems that all they talk about is the goddamn weather. You really care on Riverside Drive if there are gusty winds in the Appalachian Valley? I mean, Jesus, gimme a break.

JIM. Well, it was nice talking to you.

FRED. Look—you can hardly see Jersey—there's such a fog.

JIM. It's OK. It's a blessing . . .

FRED. Right. I don't like it any better than you do.

JIM. Actually I'm joking—I'm being—

FRED. Frivolous? . . . Flippant?

JIM. Mildly sarcastic.

FRED. It's understandable.

JIM. It is?

FRED. Knowing how I feel about Montclair.

JIM. How would I know how you feel about Montclair?

FRED. I won't even bother to comment on that.

JIM. Er—yeah—well—I'd like to get back to my thoughts.

(Looks at watch.)

FRED. What time you expect her?

JIM. What are you talking about? Please leave me alone.

FRED. It's a free country. I can stay here and stare at New Jersey if I want.

JIM. Fine. But don't talk to me.

FRED. Don't answer.

JIM. *(Takes out cell phone.)* Hey look, do you want me to call the police?

FRED. And tell them what?

JIM. That you're harassing me—aggressive panhandling.

FRED. Suppose I took that cell phone and tossed it right into the river. Twenty minutes it'd be carried off into the Atlantic. Of course, if the current ran the other way it'd wind up in Poughkeepsie. Do I mean Poughkeepsie or Tarrytown?

JIM. *(A bit scared and angry.)* I've been to Tarrytown in case you were going to ask me that next.

FRED. Where'd you stay there?

JIM. Pocantico Hills. I used to live there. Is that OK with you?

FRED. Now they call it Sleepy Hollow—sounds better for the tourists.

JIM. Uh-huh.

FRED. Cash in on all that Ichabod Crane crap. Rip Van Winkle. It's all packaging.

JIM. Look—I was deep in thought—

FRED. Hey—we're talking literature. You're a writer.

JIM. How do you know that?

FRED. C'mon—it's me.

JIM. Are you going to tell me you can tell because of my costume?

FRED. You're in costume?

JIM. It's the tweed jacket and the corduroys, right?

FRED. Jean-Paul Sartre said that after the age of thirty a man is responsible for his own face.

JIM. Camus said that.

FRED. Sartre.

JIM. Camus. Sartre said a man assumes the traits of his occupation—a waiter will gradually walk like a waiter—a bank clerk gestures like one—because they want to become things.

FRED. But you're not a thing.

JIM. I try not to be.

FRED. Because it's safe to be a thing—because things don't perish. Like *The Wall*—the men being executed want to become one with the wall they're put up in front of—to lose themselves in the stone—to become solid, permanent, to endure, in other words, to live, to be alive.

JIM. *(Considers him—then.)* I'd love to discuss this with you another time.

FRED. Good, when?

JIM. Right now I'm a little busy . . .

FRED. Well, when? You want to have lunch, I'm free all week.

JIM. I don't really know.

FRED. I wrote a funny thing based on Irving.

JIM. Irving who?

FRED. Washington Irving—remember? We had talked about Ichabod Crane.

JIM. I didn't know we were back on that.

FRED. The headless horseman is doomed to ride the country-side, holding his head under his arm. He was a German soldier killed in the war.

JIM. A Hessian.

FRED. So he rides right into an all-night drugstore and the head says—I have a terrible headache—and the druggist says, here, take these two Extra Strength Excedrin—and the body pays for them and helps the head take two. And then we cut to them later in the night, riding over a bridge, and the head says, I feel great—

the headache is gone—I'm a new man—and then the body begins to get sad and thinks how unlucky he is because if he gets a backache, he can't find relief, not being attached to the head—

JIM. How can the body think anything?

FRED. Nobody's going to ask that question.

JIM. Why not? It's obvious.

FRED. That's why. That's why you're good at construction and dialogue but you lack inspiration. That's why you have to rely on me. Although it was a pretty sleazy thing to do.

JIM. Do what? What are you talking about?

FRED. I'm talking about money—some kind of payment and a credit of some sort.

JIM. Look, I'm meeting someone.

FRED. I know, I know, she's late.

JIM. You don't know and mind your own business.

FRED. All right—you're meeting a broad—you want to be alone? Let's get the business end of it out of the way and I'm off.

JIM. What business?

FRED. In a minute you're gonna tell me this whole thing is Kafkaesque.

JIM. It's worse than Kafkaesque.

FRED. Really? Is it—postmodern?

JIM. What do you want?

FRED. A percentage and a credit on your movie. I realize it's too late for a credit on the prints that are already in distribution, but I should have a royalty on those and a cut and my name on all subsequent prints. Not fifty percent but something fair.

JIM. Are you nuts? Why should I give you anything?

FRED. Because I gave you the idea.

JIM. You gave me?

FRED. Well—you took it from me—

JIM. I took your idea?

FRED. And you sold your first film script—and the movie seems like a success and I want what's due me.

JIM. I didn't take your idea.

FRED. Jim, let's not play games.

JIM. Let's not you play games and don't call me Jim.

FRED. OK—James. Written by James L. Swain—but everyone calls you Jim.

JIM. How do you know what everyone calls me?

FRED. I see it, I hear it.

JIM. Where? What are you talking about?

FRED. Jim Swain—Central Park West and Seventy-eighth—BMW— license plate JIMBO ONE—talk about vanity plates . . . Jimmy Connors is Jimbo One, not you—and I've seen you trying to hit a tennis ball so don't try and con me.

JIM. Have you been following me?

FRED. That mousey brunette—that's Lola?

JIM. My wife's hardly mousey!

FRED. OK, "mousey" was the wrong word—she's—not rodentine exactly—

JIM. She's a beautiful woman.

FRED. It's all very subjective.

JIM. Who the hell do you think you are?

FRED. I'd never say it to her face.

JIM. I'm her husband and I love her.

FRED. Then why are you cheating?

JIM. What?

FRED. I think I know what the other one looks like. She's a little on the cheap side, no?

JIM. There is no other one.

FRED. Then who are you meeting?

JIM. None of your goddamn business, and if you don't get out of here I'm going to call the police.

FRED. That's the last thing you want if you're having a clandestine rendezvous.

JIM. How did you know my wife's name is Lola?

FRED. I've heard you call her Lola.

JIM. Have you been stalking me?

FRED. Do I look like a stalker?

JIM. Yes.

FRED. I'm a writer. At least I was years ago. Till my visions overtook me.

JIM. Well, your imagination is too creative for me.

FRED. I know. That's why you ripped me off.

JIM. I didn't steal your idea.

FRED. Not just my idea. It was autobiographical. So in a way you stole my life.

JIM. If there were any similarities between my film and your life, I assure you, they're coincidental.

FRED. I'm not the kind of guy who sues. Some people are litigation-prone. *(With some suggestion of menace.)* I like to settle between the parties.

JIM. How did I take your idea?

FRED. You overheard me tell the plot.

JIM. To who? Where?

FRED. Central Park.

JIM. I heard you in Central Park?

FRED. That's right.

JIM. To who? When?

FRED. To John.

JIM. Who?

FRED. John.

JIM. John who?

FRED. Big John.

JIM. Who?

FRED. Big John.

JIM. Who the hell is Big John?

FRED. I don't know—he's a homeless guy. Was. I heard he got his throat cut in a shelter.

JIM. You told some tale to a homeless man and you're saying I overheard you?

FRED. And used it.

JIM. I never saw you in my life.

FRED. Christ, I've been stalking you for months.

JIM. Stalking me?

FRED. And I know everything about you but you never even noticed me. And I'm not a little guy. I'm big. I could probably snap your neck in half with one hand.

JIM. *(Nervous.)* Look—whoever you are, I promise—

FRED. The name's Fred. Fred Savage. Good name for a writer, isn't it? For Best Original Screenplay, the envelope please—and the winners are Frederick R. Savage and James L. Swain for *The Journey.*

JIM. I wrote *The Journey.* And it was my idea.

FRED. Jim, you overheard me telling it to John Kelly. Poor John. He was walking on York Avenue and they were hoisting a piano and the rope came undone—God, it was awful . . .

JIM. You said he was knifed at a shelter.

FRED. Foolish consistency is the hobgoblin of small minds.

JIM. Look, Fred—I never stole anybody's idea. First, I don't need to because I have my own ideas, and second, I wouldn't even if I ran dry, OK?

FRED. But the story's all there. My breakdown, the straitjacket, my last-minute panic—the rubber between my teeth, then the electric shocks—my God—of course I was violent—

JIM. You're violent?

FRED. In and out.

JIM. Look, I'm starting to get a little alarmed.

FRED. Don't worry, she'll be here.

JIM. Over you, not her. OK—if you think you're a writer—

FRED. I said years ago—before my collapse—before all that unpleasantness occurred—I wrote for an agency.

JIM. Unpleasantness?

FRED. It's morbid, I don't want to relive it.

JIM. What kind of an agency?

FRED. An ad agency. I wrote commercials. Like that idea for the Extra Strength Excedrin one. It didn't fly. We ran it up the flagpole but it just didn't fly. Too Cartesian.

JIM. And you became—unhinged.

FRED. Not over that. Who cares that they reject my idea? Those gray flannel philistines. No, my problem arose from other sources.

JIM. Like what?

FRED. Like small cadres of men who had banded together to form a conspiratorial network—a network dedicated to my undoing, to my humiliation, to my defeat both physical and mental. A network so vast and complex that to this day it employs undercover agents in organizations as diverse as the CIA and the Cuban underground. Forces so malevolent that they cost me my job, my marriage, and what little bank account I had left. They trailed me, tapped my phone, and communicated in code with my psychiatrist by sending electrical signals from the top of the Empire State Building, through my inner ear, directly to his rubber raft at Martha's Vineyard. So don't give me your goddamn sob stories and deal with me like a mensch!

JIM. I'm frightened, Fred—I gotta level with you. I want to do the right thing by you—

FRED. Then do it. There's no need to be scared. I haven't been off my medicine long enough to lose control—at least I don't think I have—

JIM. What do you take?

FRED. A number of antipsychotic mixtures.

JIM. A cocktail.

FRED. Except I don't drink it out of a stemmed glass.

JIM. But you can't just go off those things—

FRED. I'm fine, I'm fine. Don't start accusing me like the others.

JIM. No, I'm not—

FRED. Let's talk turkey.

JIM. I had intended to prove to you logically I couldn't have taken your idea—

FRED. My life, my life—you stole my life.

JIM. Your life—your autobiography, whatever. I think I can show you step by step—

FRED. Logic can be very deceptive. You stole my life, you stole my soul.

JIM. I don't need your life. I have a fine life of my own.

FRED. Who are you to say you don't need my life?

JIM. I didn't mean to insult you.

FRED. Look, I realize you're under personal strain.

JIM. I am, yes.

FRED. And she's quite late—that's a bad sign.

JIM. I'm surprised. She's usually punctual.

FRED. She must sense something's up. I'd keep alert if I was you.

JIM. I am. I just want to point out that my film—

FRED. Our film—

JIM. *The* film—is it OK if I say *the* film? *The* film is about the evils of one particular mental institution which I happened to set in New Jersey.

FRED. Been there, done that.

JIM. But surely many people had similar experiences. This could be their story as easily.

FRED. No—no—you heard me tell it. I even said to Big John Kelly it would make a swell film—especially the part where the protagonist lights the fires.

JIM. Is that what happened in your life?

FRED. You know the details.

JIM. I swear I don't.

FRED. I was under instructions to burn down several buildings.

JIM. Instructions, from who?

FRED. The radio.

JIM. You heard voices over the radio?

FRED. Do I hear the barest trace of skepticism in your voice?

JIM. No—

FRED. I was not always—whatever was their term—

JIM. Paranoid schizophrenic?

FRED. What'd you say?

JIM. I was trying to be helpful.

FRED. Everyone's so damn technical. That's all semantics. It used to be dementia praecox—actually that's prettier. It's worse than semantics, it's cosmetics. A girl brings her fiancé home to meet her parents and says, folks, this is Max, he's a manic-depressive. You can imagine how they take it. Fantasies of their darling child wed to a guy who on Monday tries to jump off the Chrysler

Building and Tuesday tries to buy every item in Bloomingdale's—ah, but say, this is Max—he's bipolar. It sounds like an achievement—like an explorer—bipolar like Admiral Byrd. No, Jim—they diagnosed me in more prosaic terms. Not screwy or off his rocker—we're not talking vaudeville here—they said Fred Savage is homicidal—an unpredictable psychopath.

JIM. Homicidal?

FRED. Don't you just love labels?

JIM. Er—look, Fred, aware as you are of being delusional you can then see why I might think your theory, that I took your idea, may not be based on reality.

FRED. Who's to say what's real? Are we particles or rays? Is everything expanding or contracting? If we enter a black hole and the laws of physics are suspended, will I still need an athletic supporter?

JIM. Fred, you're obviously an educated man—

FRED. Phi Beta Kappa. Brown University. I can read Sanskrit. Ph.D. in Literature. Dissertation on the Positive Results of the Triangular Tension Between Goethe, Schopenhauer and Schopenhauer's Mother. So what was I doing in an ad agency, you ask? Having nervous breakdowns—not just because the hacks failed to see the brilliance of my Extra Strength Excedrin concept but because they were blind to the originality of my thought in general. Example: eight whores are sitting around in a brothel. A john comes in and surveys them up and down. He finally passes them all up and selects the umbrella stand in the corner. He goes down the hall with it in his arms, takes it to bed and has intense and passionate sexual intercourse with it. Cut to him driving off in a VW Beetle and we flash on the screen—Volkswagen—for the man with special taste. God, how they hated that one. By now I was in and out of institutions like I had a season ticket. And when I lost my job, my girlfriend, Henrietta, who I believe only put up with me because she had a severe disorder of her own, which might charitably be characterized as thermonuclear masochism, kicked me out. Yes, Jim—I was very upset. I wept. Salty tears descended these rubicund cheeks—and in an effort to woo her back I went searching for an appropriate offering with which to hopefully mollify her newly discovered feelings of disgust for me. Aware of her taste for antique jewelry I surmised an old pin or Victorian brooch might turn the trick, and having selected just the right one in a Third Avenue antique shop, I by chance came across a very stylish 1940s radio, perfect for my kitchen. Red plastic it was—a Philco. And when I got it home and tried it out, I was surprised to hear an announcer's voice commanding me to burn down the very ad agency I had formerly worked for. It was the most fun I've ever had. Am I losing you?

JIM. This is a very sad story.

FRED. I loved that girl, Henrietta. And while her attention deficit disorder made any conversation between us longer than forty seconds impossible, something in our contact buoyed my spirits. That's why I can empathize with your pathetic love life.

JIM. My love life is just fine.

FRED. Jim—you're talking to your writing partner.

JIM. You're not my writing partner.

FRED. You need a collaborator.

JIM. I've never collaborated in my life.

FRED. You're good at the nuts and bolts—but you need someone who can light a fire. I'm an idea man. OK, some may be a little avant-garde for Mr. and Mrs. Front Porch.

JIM. I have my own ideas.

FRED. If you did you wouldn't have swiped mine.

JIM. I didn't swipe it.

FRED. Genius is in the chromosomes. Did you know my personal DNA glows in the dark?

JIM. What makes you think I'm so uninspired?

FRED. I think you're very—professional. It's very solid—notice you do a lot of adaptations—not originals—I, on the other hand, am a true original—like Stravinsky—or ketchup. That's why my idea was the first thing you ever did that meant anything. It had juice—it had spark.

JIM. I thought of it in the shower.

FRED. *(Turning on him violently.)* Don't give me that jive! I want my half!

JIM. For Christ's sake, stay calm.

FRED. And don't tell me your love life's fine. Because what the hell are you doing sneaking around on Lola?

JIM. That's not your affair.

FRED. No, it's your affair.

JIM. I'm not having an affair.

FRED. What's wrong with Lola?

JIM. Nothing.

FRED. Apart from a certain—what is it I mean—is it a ferret?

JIM. Keep your mouth shut. You're talking about the woman I love.

FRED. What's wrong there?

JIM. Nothing.

FRED. Jim.

JIM. Nothing.

FRED. Jim, c'mon.

JIM. It was fine till we had the twins.

FRED. Right—two perfect look-alikes—a grizzly omen.

JIM. They're adorable boys.

FRED. Boys—at least twin girls you can dress cute.

JIM. They're cute—they're cuddly—they're—

FRED. Exactly identical?

JIM. So what?

FRED. And they both have Lola's gerbil-like visage?

JIM. Before they came we had a perfectly good marriage.

FRED. Says who?

JIM. I'm telling you, it was fine.

FRED. Just fine? Not great?

JIM. We shared a lot of interests.

FRED. Name two.

JIM. Weekends in Connecticut and macrobiotic food.

FRED. I'm falling asleep here.

JIM. We liked to scuba dive and discuss the great books.

FRED. You discussed books underwater?

JIM. And she plays piano and I play baritone sax.

FRED. Thank God it's not the other way around.

JIM. Go ahead—make fun of me.

FRED. What about your sex life?

JIM. That's none of your business.

FRED. Those two big front teeth of hers—do they hurt?

JIM. Why must you be a vulgar smart-ass?

FRED. I'm trying to grasp your situation. How often did you make love?

JIM. Often. Till the twins were born.

FRED. I'd say you were basically a missionary position man, am I right?

JIM. *(Annoyed)* We did our share of experimenting.

FRED. What do you call experimenting?

JIM. Why must you know?

FRED. We're a team.

JIM. *(Annoyed)* That's right. *(Slight pause.)* We had a threesome once, OK?

FRED. Who was the other woman?

JIM. It was a guy.

FRED. Are you bisexual?

JIM. I never touched him.

FRED. Whose idea was the threesome?

JIM. Hers.

FRED. I wonder why.

JIM. We'd seen it on the porn channel one night.

FRED. You watch that consistently?

JIM. Of course not. But sometimes you can get some good ideas.

FRED. Aha—so you do use other people's ideas.

JIM. And once we did it at her parents' house during the Thanksgiving dinner.

FRED. Did the other dinner guests look up from their turkey?

JIM. We were in the bathroom!

FRED. So there was a certain spontaneity.

JIM. I don't know why you think I'm so lackluster.

FRED. Did Lola have an orgasm?

JIM. I don't think I'll dignify that with an answer.

FRED. They have been known to fake it, you know.

JIM. Why on earth would she fake it?

FRED. Bolster your confidence. She doesn't want you to know you're not satisfying her.

JIM. I'm completely secure about my sexual prowess.

FRED. You know what they say.

JIM. What?

FRED. A dog doesn't see its own tail.

JIM. What the hell does that mean?

FRED. Maybe you think you're better than you are.

JIM. That's not true.

FRED. Then why would Lola fake it?

JIM. You said she faked it.

FRED. That's the message I'm getting.

JIM. What message?

FRED. From the top of the Empire State Building. I'm feeling those rays—those electrical charges from the big antenna on the Empire State Building and all those photons are saying—Lola was pretending to come.

JIM. Hey look, I'm trying to have a rational—

FRED. And then came the twins—David and Seth.

JIM. Carson and Django.

FRED. Really?

JIM. Lola's a big fan of Carson McCullers—

FRED. And you play jazz so—

JIM. So they *weren't* conventional names.

FRED. And you love them.

JIM. I'm crazy about them. But Lola's too crazy about them. Suddenly everything changed—it all became about the twins— there was never any time for me anymore—for us.

FRED. No more underwater discussions of Proust.

JIM. Naturally the sex fell off.

FRED. And you started cheating.

JIM. Yes—yes—

FRED. Hmmm . . . that explains a lot. Look—take my advice, call it quits with your mistress—it can only lead to heartache.

JIM. I don't need your advice. That's what I planned to do today. If she ever gets here.

FRED. Maybe she senses you want it over so she's not coming.

JIM. She doesn't have a clue. She'll be stunned.

FRED. Oh great, I think I'll stick around and watch this.

JIM. What the hell am I doing having an affair? Six lousy months of dark restaurants, dingy bars, and cheap hotel rooms. Not to mention the furtive phone calls and the tension and self-hate.

FRED. What does your psychiatrist say?

JIM. He said stop.

FRED. And you—

JIM. I stopped—seeing the psychiatrist.

FRED. It's just as well, most of them have hidden tape recorders.

JIM. Last night I came home and I saw Lola sitting on the sofa, curled up like—like—

FRED. A tiny guinea pig?

JIM. I wasn't going to say that. Like a sweet, decent woman who's been my closest friend my whole life.

FRED. Did you ever lead this woman on? Make any promises, tell her you loved her or that you might leave your wife?

JIM. Absolutely not—in no way—not for a second.

FRED. I don't know why, but I'm sensing a vibration that says maybe you did.

JIM. That's nonsense.

FRED. Um, I don't know . . .

JIM. She wanted me to go to the Caribbean with her—for five days. I was to lie to Lola and say it was a business trip.

FRED. And you agreed?

JIM. Not exactly—I said I'd think about it. It was a moment of weakness. Our clothes were off and I'd had three margaritas and there was so much salt on the rim of the glasses and I'm on a salt-free diet . . . So I suddenly got a sodium rush.

FRED. *(Folding paws downward in front of him, mimicking LOLA.)* But when you got home and saw your precious darling . .

JIM. Exactly—it was at the moment I was supposed to lie that I knew that I loved Lola despite all our problems and I was a fool.

FRED. This could get ugly.

JIM. Nothing's getting ugly. She's an adult and I'm an adult.

FRED. You said she was headstrong.

JIM. I never said any such thing.

FRED. I heard some voice say it, I *thought* it was yours.

JIM. Look, these things happen. People break off their affairs every day—don't they?

FRED. So that's why you picked such a secluded spot— you're anticipating a scene.

JIM. Hey look—why am I discussing women with you? Your view of everything is skewed.

FRED. I was married once.

JIM. *You* were?

FRED. I don't remember much about it—all that AC/DC through my head plays havoc with your memory but I do recall she was forever dialing 911.

JIM. You know what? Here's what I think—

FRED. Come in.

JIM. I think you should just leave and get back on your medicine. I'm not fooling—I'd say megadoses if possible—I don't want you around here when she comes, I can manage by myself.

FRED. OK, fine. Then let's settle our business and I'm history.

JIM. What business? We have no business. I didn't steal your idea.

FRED. Maybe on the next one you could make it up to me with an adjusted fee and top billing.

JIM. There is no next one. I don't collaborate. I work alone. I—oh—*(Notices BARBARA approaching.)* Oh oh...oh...oh...walk-away...go, go...

FRED. You're all white.

JIM. She's coming.

FRED. All right, don't panic.

JIM. You got me so distracted.

FRED. All I said was I think you're in for rough going.

JIM. Why do you say that?

FRED. Empire State Building.

JIM. No, it's going to be fine. 1 practiced my speech in the shower. I was in there an hour and a half. I know exactly what I'm going to say. Get out of here!

(BARBARA is there now.)

BARBARA. Sorry I'm late. Who's this?

JIM. Oh—I don't know . . .

(JIM gesturing with his head, trying to signal FRED to leave.)

BARBARA. Are you having a neck spasm?

JIM. *(Hands FRED money.)* Er—here's the buck you asked for, fella, go get a square meal—good luck, buddy . . . ha, ha . . .

FRED. Fred. Fred Savage. I'm a friend of Jim's.

BARBARA. You didn't say anything—

JIM. He's kidding.

FRED. I'm his writing partner.

BARBARA. Writing partner?

FRED. We collaborated on *The Journey*—it was my idea—he did the actual screenplay. *(Calling off.)* Come in.

BARBARA. What? What's going on?

FRED. Tell her, Jim.

BARBARA. Tell me what?

JIM. Fred—leave us alone.

FRED. I'm afraid you'll pussyfoot.

BARBARA. Jim, is something wrong?

FRED. The best way is to be direct.

JIM. Get out of here, Fred.

FRED. Barbara, Jim has something to tell you.

BARBARA. About what? What is this?

FRED. About your extramarital affair.

JIM. Fred's crazy—he's a street lunatic.

FRED. Tell her, Jim, or I will.

BARBARA. What's going on here?

JIM. This is none of your business.

BARBARA. I didn't know you had a writing partner.

JIM. I don't.

FRED. I'm the idea man, Jim handles the construction and dialogue. Although I'm not bad at dialogue. I wrote a great copy line once for these wonderful Japanese air conditioners—

JIM. Fred—

FRED. "They're sleek, they're silent, they'll freeze your ass off." Company would not go for it.

JIM. Let's go someplace where we can be alone.

FRED. He can't go to the Caribbean, Barbara—too attached to his wife.

BARBARA. Jim—

FRED. He wanted to tell Lola but when it came time to confront her the boy lost his resolve.

BARBARA. I don't believe this.

JIM. Barbara, try and understand.

BARBARA. Is this true? Is everything off?

JIM. I can't do it, Barbara, I've made a decision.

BARBARA. One minute you're all over me, making plans, talking big—

JIM. It was your idea. I never wanted to go away.

BARBARA. So you're through using me and now it's back to Lola.

JIM. I wasn't using you. We both knew what we were doing every step of the way.

BARBARA. You think you can just manipulate me like one of those characters in your scripts?

JIM. I sensed it was becoming too hot and heavy, so before it got totally out of control—

BARBARA. I'm sorry, Jim—it is out of control. I want to talk to Lola.

JIM. Talk to Lola?

BARBARA. Yes. I think once she hears it from me she'll get the picture.

(Pauses, looks around hopelessly.)

JIM. *(Calling off.)* Come in.

BARBARA. I don't believe you love her more than me. I'm going to meet with her and have this out.

JIM. *(To FRED.)* Say something, you're my collaborator!

FRED. I'm just the idea man, you do the dialogue.

JIM. I need a fresh concept.

FRED. Look, Barbara—may I call you Barbara?

BARBARA. I don't know who the hell you are but take a hike.

FRED. My name is Frederick R. Savage and although it does not appear on the screen or the products, I coauthored Jim's first movie and am also the inventor of the cordless phone and instant coffee.

JIM. Fred—for Christ's sake!

FRED. *(Calling off.)* Yes? Come in.

BARBARA. Promises were made to me.

JIM. Never—just the opposite—

FRED. Try and empathize, Barbara—a weak individual—a domestic crisis—a sexual impasse—suddenly an alluring creature such as yourself—the boy is of course swept away—he has fantasies, he gets lost—then one night he sees his family and is overcome by a flood of memories—guilt pervades his every pore—that same night a small spacecraft from the star Vega sends out magnetic rays which lodge inside his skull—

JIM. Fred, you're not helping me.

BARBARA. I'm sorry, Jim—it wasn't Lola you were thinking of all those nights we were locked in each other's arms.

JIM. You misread the situation—or I did—I've made a terrible mistake, I'd like to undo it—

BARBARA. I'm all shaken up—I have to rethink my plans. One thing is for certain though—I'm not some patsy who's going to roll over and play dead. You're gonna have to make this up to me somehow.

JIM. What does that mean?

BARBARA. I need time to think—but you're not walking out of this scot-free. You know what they say—if you can't get love, get money.

JIM. That's blackmail.

BARBARA. You should've thought of that when you first checked us into that fleabag hotel—now I'm calling the shots. You'll hear from me.

(BARBARA exits.)

FRED. I know what you're thinking—it all worked so great in the shower.

JIM. Fred—Fred—what do I do?

FRED. One thing is for sure—you can't pay her anything.

JIM. No?

FRED. You'd never be rid of her—she'd come back for more and more—she'd bleed you white—your kids might even have to go to public school.

JIM. I have to tell Lola—I have to—it's the only way—

FRED. It is?

JIM. It's better coming from me than from a malicious stranger.

FRED. Really?

JIM. Plus it puts an end to her threat of blackmail.

FRED. You can't tell Lola you've been having an affair for six months.

JIM. Why not? If I bring her flowers—

FRED. There's not enough flowers in the Botanical Gardens.

JIM. People have affairs and then realize they did wrong.

FRED. You're being too rational. Lola's got zero tolerance for infidelity. It was the bane of her childhood.

JIM. How do you know?

FRED. My dog told me.

JIM. I'll tell her it meant nothing. A little sexual fling.

FRED. Great. Wives love to hear that—she'll smile warmly and then serve you with papers.

JIM. What if I denied it? It'd be my word against some hysterical stranger. Who'd Lola believe?

FRED. Come in!

JIM. I'm dead—it's over. There is no way out of this. I sinned and I'm going to hell.

FRED. Hold on a second—I'm starting to pick up a radio signal . . . I feel the rays entering my head.

JIM. 1 don't need rays—I need a creative idea. For Christ's sake, we're both writers—

FRED. So much damn static . . .

JIM. Unless I just pay her off.

FRED. This weather is bad for transmission.

JIM. What have I done? The sins of the father are visited on the children.

FRED. It's so annoying.

JIM. We could move—get a motor home—we could travel around—she'd never find us.

FRED. Someone must be cooking with a microwave.

JIM. No, that's not going to work—I'm damned no matter what I do.

FRED. Wait, wait—got it! Got it!

JIM. Got what, Fred?

FRED. The solution to your problem has registered on my cortex on Gamma Channel 2000.

JIM. Great—my head doesn't get cable.

FRED. You have to get rid of her.

JIM. Uh-huh—that's your insight?

FRED. No. I mean, get rid of her definitively.

JIM. What do you mean?

FRED. My voice says, permanent elimination.

JIM. Fine—but how, short of killing her? I can't think of any other way—I—*(Realizes that's what FRED means.)* Fred—I'm trying to have a serious discussion here.

FRED. I'm very serious.

JIM. What serious? Kill her?

FRED. It's the only way you can keep your family from coming apart.

JIM. You've been off your medication too long.

FRED. I'm getting a green signal which is the go-ahead.

JIM. Fred, I'm not going to kill her.

FRED. No?

JIM. It's psychotic—you're a psychotic.

FRED. And you're just neurotic—so there's a lot I can teach you. I outrank you.

JIM. It's no solution—and if it was a solution I couldn't do it and if I could do it, I wouldn't do it.

FRED. Why not? It's a stroke of creative genius.

JIM. It's psychologically, morally, and intellectually wrong. It's madness.

FRED. It's a leap into the unthinkable.

JIM. Let it remain unthought.

FRED. The question is how to best do it.

JIM. That's not the question.

FRED. I wouldn't want you to get caught. New York has the death penalty now. I don't think it would help your cause much to be on the receiving end of one of those lethal injections.

JIM. No, I'd like to avoid that too. Fred—

FRED. We've got to act fast. This woman is an alien—she may even be computerized.

JIM. I don't want to discuss this.

FRED. If you don't give in to all her demands she'll tell Lola every detail. Lola loves you, trusts you—so she had a little post-partum obsession with the twins—I'm sure it'll pass and you'll be back having sex every Thanksgiving.

JIM. It's too radical—you're too radical.

FRED. And you're too reasonable. See, when all avenues lead to a dead end, I make the leap.

JIM. Yes—you make the leap but I get the injection.

FRED. You won't get caught. We'll plan it perfectly.

JIM. Caught or not, I don't want to do it. It's wrong. Thou Shalt Not Kill.

FRED. What is that, from one of your yuppie books on etiquette?

JIM. I gotta go home.

FRED. You're not going to have a home after tomorrow.

JIM. How could I have not seen that she'd be capable of this?

FRED. Because you're a lamb—a sweet middle-class lamb *with no imagination.*

JIM. I betrayed my wife.

FRED. That's right. Not to mention the effect of divorce on innocent kids. Twins yet—as if each doesn't have enough trouble going through life with an exact duplicate.

JIM. But killing her is out of the question.

FRED. How else are you going to stop her from telling Lola? How else?

JIM. I don't know—I got such a migraine.

FRED. Try acupuncture. But don't let them put the needles too close to the medulla, that's what they did with me.

JIM. Fred, please.

FRED. Where does she live?

JIM. Near Columbia. Fred—

FRED. Apartment house? Is there a doorman who'd recognize you?

JIM. Yes, there is.

FRED. What floor?

JIM. Eleven.

FRED. What about an elevator operator?

JIM. No—just a doorman.

FRED. Twenty-four hours? Probably not—

JIM. The doorman takes a break every now and then to get coffee.

FRED. If you take the back stairs . . .

JIM. He's only away about ten minutes. It's not enough time to take the stairs eleven flights, kill her and come down before he gets back.

FRED. Did she tell anyone about your affair? A friend?

JIM. It was our secret. That I know.

FRED. You'd have to stop off and buy gloves.

JIM. Naturally. All I need's my prints all over the place—I—Fred, what are we talking about here?! I'm not going to kill her.

FRED. You have to, old buddy. It's either that or bye-bye Lola and the kids.

JIM. But it's inhuman. What, I sneak up to her place?

FRED. Right.

JIM. Ring the bell.

FRED. She'll be expecting you. You'll have phoned first.

JIM. And what, strangle her?

FRED. What would you like to do, it's your choice. Strangle, smother, kitchen knife . . .

JIM. Telephone wire around the neck?

FRED. If you prefer.

JIM. Or plastic bag over the head.

FRED. Make it look like a suicide—or a robbery.

JIM. That's right—I could forge a note or better yet, get her to write one using some clever ruse. She recently lost her job at a magazine. A woman alone, depressed.

FRED. Y'know what I'm thinking—if you can get some blood that's her type, you buy a gun and bullets, you take pliers and pull the lead out of one of the bullets—you freeze her blood into a slug and force it into the cartridge shell—you enter her apartment, shoot her once in the chest—she's killed with a bullet of frozen blood—it melts in her system—same type—the cops find her dead but there's no bullet to be found. Just a hole in her body with no exit wound. *(Calling off.)* Come in.

JIM. I could drop some item in the street, get a stranger to pick it up, get his fingerprints on it. Then I could take her to one of our hotels, check in as Sam and Felicity Arbogast, kill her in the room, leave the item and sneak down the fire staircase.

FRED. I don't like the name Felicity—it's too offbeat.

JIM. It's an easy switch. Jane Arbogast.

FRED. Plus you'd be leaving a paper trail. They got these handwriting experts.

JIM. I can sign the register with my left hand.

FRED. Wait a minute—wait a minute—no, it'd never work.

JIM. What?

FRED. I was thinking if you locked her in the closet and ran a rubber tube through the keyhole and sucked the air out.

JIM. I read a story once where the guy beat someone to death with a leg of lamb and then ate the murder weapon. That is a funny one. *(Laughs)* He ate the weapon.

FRED. This is no joking matter, Jim. You're going to have to eliminate that woman and soon.

JIM. I'm not doing it, Fred. I can't.

FRED. Maybe in the end the best thing would be to call her to meet for a drink, kill her on a dark street, rob her—make it look like a mugging.

JIM. I won't do it.

FRED. On the other hand, maybe you really want your marriage to break up.

JIM. What are you saying?

FRED. Yes—get that hamster of a wife off your back and be rid of those eerie look-alike sons and all the while you can keep insisting you didn't dump *them*. It was out of your control—a jealous woman wrecked your home.

JIM. Please spare me those pseudo-Freudian insights.

FRED. Of course—you wind up a free man. A divorceé—a new life—actresses, models, discos.

JIM. That's enough.

FRED. Am I hitting on a truth?

JIM. Look, I'm not saying I'm not in a terrible predicament. I'm not saying I wouldn't be lucky if Barbara was—was—

FRED. You can say it.

JIM. Deceased. But she's a human being.

FRED. You say that like it's a good thing.

JIM. Isn't it?

FRED. I don't know. Have you ever gone to a tenants' meeting in a co-op?

JIM. Maybe I led her on without intending to. It's possible. I may be more responsible than I realize.

FRED. But you acted out of bumbling stupidity. You're starved for a little attention at home, a little passion, so you blunder into an affair where you get some pampering and some illicit sex and you go with it. Eventually you come to your senses but it's too late. A scheming woman won't let go. You're pathetic. But that's OK, most people are pathetic. See, now, I, on the other hand, am tragic.

JIM. I'm pathetic and you're tragic?

FRED. Oh yeah. I had greatness in me. A different roll of the dice and I could have been Shakespeare or Milton.

JIM. Are you kidding? With the eight whores and a Volkswagen?

FRED. You have a chance to redeem yourself. To prevent the destruction of your family by a vindictive bitch whose rage at not getting what she wants decays into blackmail.

JIM. It's morally unacceptable.

FRED. What you've done is already morally unacceptable. You've cheated on your wife, you've lied, you've broken your marriage vows.

JIM. OK—it was wrong—but it's not murder.

FRED. You say murder like it was the ultimate act. To a more creative mind like mine it's—another option.

JIM. That's the difference between us, Fred. You have delusions of grandeur. I'm more earthbound. I don't get my instructions from rays coming from the Empire State Building or a hovering spacecraft.

FRED. That can be changed—I know a brain surgeon who can install a dish.

JIM. I accept the Judeo-Christian ethic.

FRED. You take your orders from a cartel?

JIM. You equate psychosis with creativity.

FRED. Hey, don't believe me—check your reviews over the years. What do you think the critics mean when they euphemistically refer to you as a "fine craftsman"?

JIM. That I'm a solid professional. You're just unstructured madness.

FRED. That's why we'd make a good team.

JIM. No, I don't want to be a team.

FRED. You're afraid.

JIM. Maybe—but it's my choice and I'm saying no to murder. I realize there's probably going to be very painful consequences, but I'm responsible for what I've gotten myself into and if Barbara chooses to behave like a vicious snake, taking her life is still absolutely unacceptable.

FRED. We have hit on the kernel of your problem, kid. You can't make the leap.

(Now BARBARA appears on the scene again.)

BARBARA. I want to talk to you.

JIM. Barbara—I thought—

BARBARA. I'm glad you're still here.

FRED. Barbara, are you allergic to any insect sprays or roach powder?

JIM. Fred!

BARBARA. I want to speak to him alone.

FRED. Alone? How is that possible?

BARBARA. Without you around.

FRED. But we're partners.

JIM. OK, Fred—give me some space—we're not joined at the hip.

FRED. But our collaboration—

JIM. Please—I need some time with Barbara. Go chat with the mother ship.

FRED. OK—suit yourself. I'm out of here. *(Sotto to JIM.)* You see that glowing red aura around her? The only time I've ever seen it before was around Nixon.

(FRED exits.)

JIM. Barbara, I'm sorry about everything.

BARBARA. I needed a few minutes to clear my head.

JIM. You were pretty frazzled back there.

BARBARA. Everything took me by surprise.

JIM. I apologize for that. There's no easy way to end an affair.

BARBARA. I knew what I was getting myself into.

JIM. I never led you on. We're both adults.

BARBARA. I've been a little tense lately. Lost my job—been drinking a little too much.

JIM. I understand. I was going through a bad period in my marriage for a while. Maybe it'll never right itself, but having an affair is not the way I should be dealing with it. If there's anything I can do for you—

BARBARA. I'd like three hundred thousand dollars.

JIM. Just let me know.

BARBARA. Three hundred down and two more by the end of the year.

JIM. Pardon me?

BARBARA. You've come into some dough with your screenplay. I think you can manage a half mil.

JIM. Barbara, think what you're doing—

BARBARA. You think. I could make your life miserable but I'm not. That's got to be worth something.

JIM. A half million dollars—

BARBARA. You gonna quibble? I'll go to Lola right now.

JIM. I can't pay that kind of money.

BARBARA. You mean you won't.

JIM. No, I won't. Even if I could I wouldn't. Because it wouldn't stop there. You'd be all over me next year and the year after that.

BARBARA. Jim, you're not in a position to make the rules.

JIM. I'm trying to clean up a mess I made, not get deeper into it. This would tie us together forever. You'd bleed me white over the years. I'd never be free of you.

BARBARA. I want the money by tomorrow—the first payment, that is. You have twenty-four hours.

JIM. I don't need twenty-four hours.

BARBARA. If I don't hear from you by tomorrow afternoon I'll assume you'd prefer I blew the whistle. Your choice. Sleep well.

(As she goes off, JIM doesn't know where to turn, then he takes out his cellular phone.)

JIM. *(Ranting)* No—you won't blow any whistle because I will. I'll tell Lola myself. I'll confess everything. I'll beg her to understand. I'll weep, I'll grovel. Lola's a decent human. Maybe she can find it in her heart to forgive me . . . all right, that's a long shot . . . but I couldn't go on living knowing there was someone out there who could wreck my home on a whim . . . every time she wanted more money . . . and the payments would get bigger . . . bigger and more frequent . . . How would I explain that? No, Lola, we can't afford the apartment anymore—but I can't tell you why . . . And the vacation's out—and the boys have to get jobs. Little twin jobs . . . *(FRED has entered laconically and just observes JIM, who doesn't see FRED and speaks into the phone.)* Hello—Lola, it's Jim. Jim Swain . . . your—your husband . . . old Jim Swain, James Swain, ha, ha . . . So how've you been? Good—life treating you right? Ha, ha—what? No—I haven't been drinking. I just wanted to chat. You know I love you . . . ha, ha . . . Lola—I have something to tell you—

(FRED takes the cellular phone away and throws it onto the ground.)

FRED. What are you doing?

JIM. What'd you do?

FRED. You weren't going to confess everything to Lola, were you?

JIM. Yes I was—do you know that you were right about Barbara—she has a red aura around her—I'm sure I saw it—she wants five hundred thousand dollars—for openers—can you believe that? Three hundred big ones tomorrow and the rest by the end of the year. But I'm not paying it—not a nickel—not a red cent.

FRED. Not to worry. Twenty minutes and Barbara'll be in the Atlantic—or Poughkeepsie if the current ran upstream.

JIM. You don't understand, I—Fred—you didn't—

FRED. I was right about her, Jim, she takes her orders from another galaxy.

JIM. Fred, say it isn't so—

FRED. Don't worry—there's no way you can be linked to it.

JIM. Ohmigod.

FRED. Very clever. She had a computer chip implanted in her ear. She was part of a plan to enslave the Bronx.

JIM. I've got to get out of here.

FRED. If she's ever found, somewhere in the vast Atlantic—it'll look like a suicide they'll never know one way or the other. You said yourself, a woman alone, recently lost her job.

JIM. You threw her in the Hudson River?

FRED. All that elaborate planning—it was bad writing. The best plots are the simplest. I was sitting on a bench, she walked by—we were both alone—it came to me in a moment of inspiration. That's the difference between us two—with you it would have been labored and overanalyzed. This is not real, that's not logical. To me it just *felt* right.

JIM. I'm going to be sick.

FRED. Hey look, forget about the royalties from our movie—and forget about collaborating—truth is, I don't really want to be a

writer—I'd forgotten how tedious it is—it's lonely work, Jim—
and I've had an offer to be part of the next Apollo team—they're
talking about a manned mission to Alpha Centauri. But keep at
your work—you're a good professional—although I would recom-
mend eventually you find someone to team up with—there's no
shame in collaborating—it's just that you're missing a part.

JIM. I'm in a state of shock.

FRED. Keep your eye on the stars, Jim. There's life on many
of them—not that they necessarily mean us well. The object of the
Apollo mission is to explore some of the trouble spots in the universe and deal with any eventuality that may occur—the President
knows about it—we've discussed it at length . . . it's not all a bed
of roses out there . . .

(The cellular phone rings and JIM answers.)

JIM. *(Into phone.)* Hello? Lola—yes . . . I don't know what
happened . . . we were disconnected . . . Oh no . . . I was about to
say . . . I called because I miss you and I'll pick you up at work and
we can walk home together . . . I love you . . . I love you . . . I—
oh, Lola—

(Exiting as FRED rants.)

FRED. I can actually make out some canals on Neptune—they
could be decoys—what did we do to make them so angry at us?
Nothing, you say? Think again . . . You're not the type for an extramarital affair—and be thankful—the price is too dear—love to
Lola . . . Come in!

FADE OUT

*Curtain rises on a country home in Connecticut. A combination of
American antiques and contemporary furnishings—perhaps a
large stone fireplace—a staircase leading upstairs. SHEILA
and NORMAN, who live there, are hosting a barbecue out in
the back. SHEILA'S sister, JENNY, and her husband, DAVID,
are the only guests. Sound of geese honking.*
*JENNY, SHEILA and NORMAN are fixing and/or refilling drinks
while they make small talk prior to going out back to cook.*

SHEILA. *(Looks out window and says wistfully.)* Look,
Norman, the geese are back.

NORMAN. Spoken like the tragic heroine of a Russian play.

JENNY. I hate Russian plays. Nothing happens and they
charge the same price as a musical.

SHEILA. To think that each year when the geese migrate
south they pick our little pond to lay over at for a few days.

NORMAN. I told you Old Saybrook is becoming the in place.

DAVID. What do the geese tell us about the inscrutable mag-
nificence of nature?

SHEILA. What?

DAVID. That one day we all must grow old and decay. That's
the message in all of nature.

JENNY. That's easy for him to say, he's a plastic surgeon and that message is on his business card.

SHEILA. Your wife got you, David.

DAVID. *(Toasts)* To the geese.

JENNY. Not the geese—to Norman and Sheila. Happy seventh anniversary.

NORMAN. Some of the happiest years of my life. Maybe two of them. Just joking.

SHEILA. Freud said there are no jokes.

NORMAN. *(Toasts)* To Sigmund Freud—the poet of penis envy.

DAVID. And now, if you'll all excuse me, I'm going into the den to watch Tiger Woods—please don't disturb me until the steaks come off the barbecue.

(Exits to den.)

JENNY. *(Exiting, to SHEILA.)* I'll make more ice—it's one of the only things I learned in cooking school.

DAVID. *(Returning)* Where are the pistachio nuts?

SHEILA. I don't know . . .

DAVID. I can't watch golf without pistachio nuts.

SHEILA. David.

DAVID. They must be red—red, salted pistachio nuts.

SHEILA. *(Exiting to kitchen.)* I have cashews—

DAVID. Cashews are basketball. Pistachios are golf.

NORMAN. David, just get out. *(David exits into den.)* I figured out what the geese symbolize. They symbolize impending disaster—the honking is a mating call and a mating call always spells trouble.

(Bell rings.)

NORMAN. *(Calls out.)* Sheila, are you expecting anyone?

SHEILA. *(Returning to room.)* No. *(They open the door and a comparable couple, HAL and SANDY MAXWELL, stand there.)* Yes?

HAL. Hello—I hope we're not disturbing you.

SANDY. *(A bit embarrassed.)* This is silly, Hal.

HAL. I'm Hal Maxwell and this is my wife, Sandy. We were driving by and we don't want to intrude, but we used to live here.

SHEILA. Really?

SANDY. Yes—for nine years—we sold the place to a Mr. Krolian.

HAL. Max Krolian, a fairly well-known writer.

NORMAN. Sure—well, we've been here for about three years now. Norman Pollack—Sheila's my wife. Please—come in.

SANDY. We don't want to bother you. We've moved to New Jersey and we happened to be up here for one day antiquing and we were so close.

SHEILA. Please—come in. Have a look around. Feel free.

NORMAN. So you used to live here?

SHEILA. Can we offer you a drink?

HAL. Oh God—I would love one.

SANDY. You have to drive.

(They have entered in deeper and look around.)

SHEILA. How does it took?

HAL. It brings back such memories.

NORMAN. What would you like?

HAL. What I would *like* is a single malt scotch but I will drink anything.

NORMAN. And you?

SANDY. Oh, just a tiny bit of white wine if you have it.

NORMAN. We have no white but our martinis are colorless.

(SANDY laughs at NORMAN'S joke.)

HAL. *(At window.)* Whose idea was it to put in a swimming pool?

NORMAN. We did that.

HAL. What shape is it?

NORMAN. Amoeba—an amoeba . . . it's an amoeba-shaped pool.

HAL. Those little germs . . .

SANDY. Hal—

(JENNY enters.)

SHEILA. Oh—Jenny—these are—

HAL. The Maxwells.

SHEILA. They used to live here.

SANDY. We just wanted to see the place again—we were married here.

JENNY. Oh—how sweet.

HAL. In that garden. Under a maple tree now it's gone, there's a pool.

SHEILA. You hungry?

SANDY. No—

HAL. What are you telling them no, we're starved.

NORMAN. Well then, join us—we're barbecuing some steaks.

SANDY. No, we couldn't.

HAL. Er—medium rare.

DAVID. *(Emerges from den momentarily.)* Who came in? I

heard the bell ring just as Tiger was about to putt. I think the noise made him miss.

JENNY. My husband—David, this is—

HAL. Hal and Sandy Maxwell—we used to live here.

DAVID. Oh really? Where did you put the pistachio nuts?

JENNY. David, they got married here.

DAVID. Oh great. Do you play golf?

HAL. No.

DAVID. Um, terrific. We must play sometime.

JENNY. In the winter it's the Knicks, in the summer it's golf—talk about Freud—he loves to watch young men put balls in holes.

(She goes.)

HAL. Hey—what happened to the beautiful floor that was here?

NORMAN. Oh, er—we redid it.

HAL. Redid the random planking? Why?

NORMAN. We wanted something smoother.

SANDY. *(With a look to her husband.)* It's lovely—

HAL. This floor is the first spot we made love on—

SANDY. Hal—

HAL.—right here—where the coffee table is. It was smooth enough for us.

SANDY. Hal—

SHEILA. Er—that's very romantic.

HAL. I think so. Sandy gets shy. It was a memorable moment. Particularly since we were both married to different people at the time.

SANDY. Hal!

SHEILA. Oh goodness.

HAL. Don't get the wrong impression. We were drunk, here alone, there was an electrical storm, all the lights went out—suddenly the room was illuminated by a flash of lightning and I saw Sandy, her lips full, her hair wild from the intense humidity she beckoned me to her with the ever increasing promise of sexual adventure.

SHEILA. What do you do, Mr. Maxwell?

HAL. Hal. I'm an accountant. See—her face fell.

SHEILA. What?

HAL. You figured me for a poet, right? I don't seem the type to be crunching numbers for a business firm—do I?

SHEILA. I don't know—accountants can be poetic. You should see some of our tax returns.

HAL. I feel there's more in me but I just don't have the courage.

SANDY. Hal would like to write the great American novel.

HAL. Play, Sandy, play—not novel. Although I have written a few poems about the dangers of cholesterol. Sonnets.

SANDY. Did you know Mr. Krolian, the former owner?

NORMAN. Only by reputation.

HAL. I met him once when we sold the place. I tried to talk to him—he was a difficult man to communicate with—but a very clever writer.

NORMAN. Excuse me. I better go help her sister, Jenny—whenever she tries to light the barbecue we wind up on the six o'clock news.

(He goes.)

SANDY. What does your husband do, Mrs.—

SHEILA. Sheila—he's a dentist.

HAL. Hey, that's almost as bad as me—ooh—well, I mean—er—what does your sister do? Is she a model?

SHEILA. Jenny has a lingerie shop in Manhattan, and her husband streamlines rear ends and I don't mean automotive work. He's a plastic surgeon.

(SANDY laughs at SHEILA'S joke.)

SANDY. *(Looking out window.)* The birdhouse is still up.

HAL. I designed and built that birdhouse myself.

SANDY. Based on the Guggenheim.

HAL. Hey—do you know about the secret vault?

SHEILA. No.

HAL. Yes, we wouldn't have known except we were told by the original owner who built the house, Mr. Warner. He made a hidden safe behind the fireplace.

SHEILA. No.

HAL. Yes—he did—

SANDY. Show her.

HAL. Here, it's right behind here, but you have to know where the hidden latch is.

(Fiddling)

SANDY. It's the top one and you pull the lever . . .

HAL. Here it—I got it—here you go . . .

SHEILA. *(Watches it open.)* My God, you learn something new every day—

HAL. I can't believe you didn't know about it.

SHEILA. I had no idea! I lean on that mantel all the time—I never dreamed—a hidden safe—what's this?

SANDY. What is that?

SHEILA. *(Removes an old notebook—reads aloud.)* I want to treasure these moments because they are the most passionate I've known. *(Looks up.)* Hmm. What is this? *(Thumbs diary—reads.)* Her quivering breasts under my hands caused us both to breathe heavy—

HAL. What'd you find there?

SHEILA. *(Reads)* Chronicle of my love affair with Sheila's sister, Jenny, by Norman Pollack—

(SHEILA looks up.)

HAL. Norman Pollack—that's her husband.

SANDY. Well, it was nice meeting you . . .

SHEILA. Norman, can you come into the living room for a minute?

SANDY. We'll just let ourselves out . . .

NORMAN. *(Returning)* Did you say something, sweetheart?

SHEILA. You miserable duplicitous son of a bitch.

NORMAN. Pardon me?

(Realizes she's found something.)

SANDY. We love what you've done with the place—

SHEILA. This is yours.

NORMAN. What are you talking about?

HAL. She found your diary. You're in tremendous trouble.

NORMAN. My what? You must be kidding.

SHEILA. It's your name.

NORMAN. Oh Jesus, Sheila. There must be a hundred Norman Pollacks in the phone book.

SHEILA. This is your handwriting.

NORMAN. Lots of people dot their i's with little circles.

SHEILA. There's a snapshot of you and Jenny with your hands on her breasts.

NORMAN. That's the only real piece of evidence you have.

SHEILA. *(Reads from diary.)*
I can no longer suppress the torrid feelings I have for Sheila's sister. Making love with Jenny is an ecstasy I have never experienced with anyone else.

SANDY. If you're ever in Nutley . . .

NORMAN. How did you find it?

HAL. When we bought the place I knew about the safe.

SANDY. Shut up, Hal.

NORMAN. *You* told her about it?

HAL. How did I know you were knocking off Jenny?

NORMAN. Now, Sheila, before you jump to any conclusions . . .

HAL. Norman, you don't get it—this is the smoking gun.

SANDY. Will you shut up, Hal?

SHEILA. *(Reads from diary.)* I secretly slid my hand under her skirt as the four of us sat on the lawn at Tanglewood under the moonlight. For a moment I thought Sheila noticed—

HAL. Does it say what else happens?

NORMAN. Would you stay out of this!?

SHEILA. Today Jenny pretended she was a little girl and I slapped her rear end. She found it very erotic and we made love.

HAL. If I could just see the diary for a minute.

SANDY. Hal, butt out.

JENNY. *(Enters)* Norman—I accidentally let the fire go out in the barbecue.

SHEILA. Oh, "I accidentally let the fire go out in the barbecue"? Well, aren't you a bad little girl. Norman's going to have to give you another spanking.

JENNY. *(Doesn't get it.)* What?

NORMAN. She found my diary.

JENNY. Your what?

SHEILA. *(Reading)* Today Jenny and I met at her place and made love in the same bed she shares with David.

JENNY. You keep a diary?

NORMAN. It was completely hidden. Till he told her where to find it.

HAL. How was I to know you were banging him? I innocently showed her the safe.

JENNY. Why in hell would you keep a diary?

HAL. They're very useful for tax purposes.

SANDY. Well—I'm sure you'll work things out—now, if you'll excuse—

SHEILA. Like hell—you stay right here—you're witnesses.

HAL. Witnesses? Is something gonna happen where you need witnesses?

SHEILA. How long have you two been cheating?

NORMAN. I'd hardly call a few rendezvous cheating.

SHEILA. *(Looking in diary.)* According to this you had sexual relations four times on President's Day alone.

NORMAN. Well, yes, because Washington and Lincoln's birthdays are celebrated together.

HAL. I don't see what the big deal is here. Everybody in suburbia cheats.

SANDY. They do?

SHEILA. *(Reading diary.)* Where did you learn those positions?

JENNY. Pilates.

HAL. *(Laughing at her joke too hard.)* Did you hear that—

SANDY. I heard her, I heard her. We lived in suburbia—right

here in fact—I hope you didn't cheat, because I didn't.

HAL. Of course I wouldn't.

SANDY. Then why would you say something like that?

HAL. I was generalizing.

SANDY. Never with Holly?

HAL. Holly Fox? Gimme a break. Because she was an actress?

SANDY. Exactly—because you always insisted she wasn't so beautiful, but on several occasions you said her name in your sleep.

HAL. You're projecting because you always had a little crush on her brother.

SANDY. Believe me, if I wanted Ken Fox I would have had no problem.

HAL. Meaning what?

SANDY. Meaning he hit on me once a week for a year but I fended him off.

HAL. Well, this is the first I'm hearing about that.

SHEILA. How long have you two been having this tempestuous affair?

NORMAN. *(Simultaneously with Jenny.)* Not long.

JENNY. Three years.

NORMAN. Six months.

JENNY. A year.

NORMAN. And a half.

JENNY. Not long.

NORMAN. There was a lot of downtime.

SHEILA. How could you do it, you're my sister!

JENNY. What can I say, we fell in love.

NORMAN. It wasn't love, it was pure sex.

JENNY. You said it was love.

NORMAN. I never actually used that word—I said I "care"

for you—I "miss" you—I "need" you—I "can't live without you"—but not love.

SHEILA. All this time you've been sharing my bed you've been sleeping with Jenny.

NORMAN. Can I help it if she seduced me?

JENNY. I seduced you?

NORMAN. Three years ago I walked into her lingerie shop—to buy you a present—I found something that looked nice—I asked if it would fit you—she said she was about your size, she'd try it on—I could see it—we both went into the changing booth—she slipped into it—

HAL. Into what?

NORMAN. A thong—she was wearing a thong.

SANDY. *(To HAL.)* Will you butt out.

HAL. I'm trying to follow the narrative.

SANDY. You find her attractive, don't you?

SHEILA. You too?

HAL. What?

SANDY. I heard you ask Sheila if her sister was a model—and you've been champing at the bit to get your hands on that diary.

HAL. Can I help it if I'm an inadvertent participant in this all-too-human drama?

SHEILA. *(Handing him diary.)* Here—you appreciate literature—

HAL. I really don't—

(Has accepted diary and becomes riveted by it.)

SANDY. Oh go ahead, Hal, take it. I'm sure you'll find the details of her sexual activities gratifying.

HAL. *(Leafing through book.)* Well, maybe to—uh—uh—

SANDY. Let's say to a live male under ninety.

HAL. Gee, Sandy, I only wish you were half as adventurous as she is.

SANDY. Over my dead body.

HAL. I'm not discussing our sex life.

SANDY. I'm sorry if I disappoint you.

HAL. Look, we've been through it . . . I'm only saying, if you were willing to experiment once in a while . . .

SANDY. If by experimenting you mean a threesome with Holly Fox.

HAL. Well, what is your idea of an experiment?

SANDY. I don't think about experimenting. We're making love, not working on a science grant.

SHEILA. You always read about those perverted dentists who have sex with their unconscious patients during root canal.

NORMAN. I'm not a perverted dentist. I'm a perverted ortho-dontist—you never got that straight. Look, I take full responsibility. If you have to blame someone, blame me.

SHEILA. Who the hell do you think I'm blaming?

DAVID. *(Emerges from den.)* Tiger Woods just bogeyed a hole.

HAL. So did Norman.

DAVID. It's very exciting.

SHEILA. Join us, David, we have something to show you.

DAVID. Can't it wait?

SHEILA. I don't know, it's very hot.

JENNY. Stop being so vicious.

SHEILA. Come sit with me for a moment, David.

HAL. Quick, Sandy—do you have our camcorder?

SANDY. It's in the car.

SHEILA. Read this diary, David—see if you recognize any of

the protagonists.

DAVID. *(Taking diary.)* What is this? Tiger Woods is going to set a record.

NORMAN. Let the man enjoy his golf. This doesn't concern him.   .

HAL. Oh, Norman—he's bound to have some marginal interest.

(DAVID reads.)

SHEILA. What do you think, David—recognize the lead characters?

HAL. Of course he does.

DAVID. The people?

SHEILA. Yes, the married woman called Jenny and the dentist.

DAVID. The married woman, Jenny? Where would I recognize her from?

SHEILA. Try breakfast.

DAVID. What is this, some silly piece of porn? Why should I read it, I'm watching the U.S. Open.

SHEILA. You're married to the U.S. Open.

NORMAN. Jenny—

SHEILA. Norman!

NORMAN. Sheila.

DAVID. What? What am I missing?

HAL. Can I give him a hint?

SANDY. Will you keep out.

HAL. I can't believe he can't get it.

SHEILA. You find it a coincidence the man's name is Norman and the woman's is Jenny?

DAVID. No—why?

SHEILA. Your wife's name is Jenny, my husband's name is Norman.

DAVID. So?

SANDY. This guy's a doctor?

SHEILA. You recognize the two people in this photo?

NORMAN. Sheila—

HAL. I've heard of denial—

DAVID. Yes—that's your husband with some woman.

SHEILA. Uh-huh—you see Norman's tongue?

DAVID. Yes.

SHEILA. Where is it?

DAVID. In his mouth.

SHEILA. The other end.

DAVID. In this woman's ear.

SHEILA. And his hands?

DAVID. *(Studies photo.)* Hmmm—Norman, is this some new dental procedure?

SHEILA. And you don't recognize the woman?

DAVID. She's definitely familiar.

SHEILA. Shall I give you a clue?

JENNY. I can't stand this.

SHEILA. Remember how years ago you met a young woman at a dinner party and you hit it off and began dating?

DAVID. Yes—and we both loved Tolstoy and French films and sailing—and I married her—Jenny—so what is your point? That the woman in the diary—in the photo—resembles Jenny? That the woman resembles Jenny? That the woman resembles Jenny? That the woman resembles Jenny? That the woman—that the woman's Jenny—it's Jenny—I got it—I got it.

HAL. I'd never let this guy do my plastic surgery.

JENNY. You're so cruel, Sheila.

DAVID. *(Stunned)* This *is* you—you're her—she's you—she's who you are—

JENNY. David, try and understand—apart from the sex it was platonic.

HAL. What is the problem here? If she can discuss Tolstoy and foreign films and also does all this you've hit the jackpot.

SANDY. You have a thing for her—I felt that right off.

HAL. All I'm saying is that in addition to a cultivated wife and good mother it's nice if you go to bed each night with a real freak.

SANDY. I don't believe I'm hearing this.

DAVID. I'm stunned—I'm stupefied. I didn't even know— who is the guy again?

SHEILA. Norman—Norman—right here.

NORMAN. Oh stop it, Sheila. I've been having an affair with Jenny.

DAVID. Jenny—a woman with the same name as my wife?

SHEILA. The trauma's too much.

DAVID. A love affair?

HAL. This guy kills me—what other kind of affair is there?

DAVID. But that means Norman and Jenny are sleeping with each other.

JENNY. Yes, David, we slept together—but if it's any consolation, there was very little foreplay.

SHEILA. That sounds like Norman.

DAVID. But he's my brother-in-law and she's my wife. And who are the people in the picture?

SHEILA. He's lost it.

DAVID. Excuse me.

(Exits.)

HAL. If he's going to see Tiger Woods now, that's what I call a sports fan.

SHEILA. Of course this means a divorce.

JENNY. Sheila, I may have cheated physically, but mentally I've been a loyal sibling.

SHEILA. Sibling? How dare you? You're no longer my sister. From this moment on, the most you could ever be to me is a niece.

NORMAN. Sheila, Sheila . . . how can I make this up to you?

SHEILA. The firm of Rifkin and Abramowitz will let you know.

DAVID. *(Enters with rifle.)* And now—prepare to die.

JENNY. David!

NORMAN. All right, let's not play games. That's a loaded shotgun.

DAVID. Back off, Norman! Back off! Everybody in this room is going to die and then I'm putting the barrel in my mouth and squeezing the trigger.

HAL. *(Looks at watch.)* Oh, is it six already? We have tickets to *Mamma Mia!*

DAVID. Not so fast, I said everybody.

HAL. We just drove up to see the house.

JENNY. David, you have that look in your eye.

DAVID. First you and Norman, then Sheila.

SHEILA. Why me? What the hell did I do? I got cheated on like you.

DAVID. You found the diary.

SHEILA. He showed me where.

DAVID. Believe me, he's going too.

SANDY. We're innocent bystanders.

DAVID. That makes the news story perfect, doesn't it? The adulterous couple, the poor husband and wife—two perfectly innocent bystanders.

HAL. You're crazy.

DAVID. That's what they said about the Son of Sam.

HAL. Yes—so—they were right.

JENNY. He's flipped out.

HAL. But you can't kill *us*—we didn't do anything. I never cheated. I could have—and believe me, I wanted to.

SANDY. You did?

HAL. Well, face it, Sandy, you can be a cold fish.

SANDY. Me?

HAL. That's right—she is the opposite of Jenny—will not ever try anything new.

SANDY. Well, maybe if you'd romance me once in a while instead of doing everything so fast.

HAL. I'm only trying to get it done before the headache sets in.

DAVID. Shut up! Who let them in?! It's unfortunate you wandered in, but that's life—full of ironies—some of them pleasant, some rather ugly—I've never thought life was a gift—it's a burden—a sentence—cruel and unusual punishment—everybody say your prayers—*(They huddle together as he cocks his shotgun. Suddenly they hear a noise and a man comes down the stairs. The man is tied up and gagged, apparently having gotten loose from a chair. His arms are still tied and he makes muffled, gagged sounds.)*

DAVID. (*Noticing him.*) Oh no—

SHEILA. Oh Christ.

NORMAN. I thought—

SHEILA. Oh brother.

JENNY. Help! Help!

(HAL and SANDY— one or both run to the man and take off his gag.)

DAVID. Don't do that—don't—oh—

MAX. OK—the party's over.

SANDY. Who are you?

JENNY. Who tied him up?

DAVID. It was Norman.

SHEILA. This sinks us.

HAL. Aren't you Mr. Krolian? I'm Hal Maxwell. I sold you this house a few years ago. Sandy, it's Max Krolian—

MAX. *(Referring to ropes)* Get these off me.

HAL. *(Untying him.)* What's going on?

MAX. These wild animals—I created them—then they turned on me.

DAVID. Ah, you're incompetent.

MAX. They're from my pen.

SANDY. What is this?

JENNY. The game's up—why don't you tell 'em the truth?

HAL. What?

NORMAN. He had an idea for a play—which he was writing—

SHEILA. He invented us.

DAVID. From his fertile imagination.

SHEILA. He wrote half the play.

MAX. That's right—and I couldn't figure out where I was going with it—it wasn't coming—

DAVID. He was blocked.

MAX. Sometimes an idea seems great, but after you work on it for a while it just doesn't go anyplace.

SHEILA. But by then it was too late. We were born.

DAVID. Invented.

MAX. Created. I had half a play.

HAL. You always had a flair for creating wonderful live characters with fascinating problems and great dialogue.

NORMAN. So then what does he do?

JENNY. He gave up the idea.

NORMAN. He threw the half-finished play in the drawer.

DAVID. It's dark in the drawer.

MAX. What else could I do? I had no finish.

DAVID. I hated the goddamned drawer.

SHEILA. I mean, picture you and your wife in a drawer.

JENNY. There's nothing to do in a drawer.

NORMAN. It sucks.

SHEILA. Then Jenny got the idea that we push it open and escape into the world.

MAX. I thought I heard the drawer opening— by the time I turned around they were all over me.

SANDY. What did you think you'd do once you broke out?

SHEILA. We hoped we could figure out some way to finish his third act.

NORMAN. So we could have a life every night in theatres— forever.

JENNY. What's the alternative? To be half-finished in a dark drawer?

DAVID. I'm not going back in the drawer! I'm not going back in the drawer! I'm not going—

(NORMAN slaps DAVID.)

MAX. I've thought and thought—I can't figure where it goes.

HAL. Well, let's analyze what we've got . . . she discovers her sister is having an affair with her husband.

MAX. Who are you?

HAL. Hal Maxwell—I sold you— ˙

MAX. The accountant?

HAL. I've always wanted to write a play.

MAX. So does everyone.

HAL. Why are they having an affair? What's wrong with their marriage?

NORMAN. I'm bored with Sheila.

SHEILA. Why?

NORMAN. I don't know.

MAX. Don't ask me. I'm written out.

HAL. Why does any husband get bored with his wife? Because with time they get too familiar. The excitement wanes— they're always together around the house—they see each other undressed—there's no more mystery—now even his secretary is sexier to him—or the next-door neighbor.

JENNY. That's not realistic.

HAL. How would you know? You're not even well written. It's very realistic—it happens all the time. Take it from me.

SANDY. It does?

HAL. I mean, freshness in marriage has to be worked on— otherwise, there's no music in a relationship, and music is every-thing.

SANDY. What if the husband was once romantic but he grad-ually takes the wife for granted? What used to be a relationship full of imaginative, charming surprises is now just a life together by the numbers, with them having sex but not making love.

HAL. I'd hardly find that a believable conflict.

SANDY. I think many women would identify with it.

HAL. Too far-out.

SHEILA. I think it sounds very plausible.

JENNY. Very close to the bone.

SANDY. Very.

DAVID. And you think it can just evaporate? Even if at one time they loved one another?

MAX. That's one of the sad truths of existence. Nothing in this world is permanent. Even the characters created by the great Shakespeare will, in millions of years, cease to exist—when the universe runs its course and the lights go out.

DAVID. Jesus, I think I'll just go back and watch Tiger Woods. The hell with it all.

NORMAN. That's right. What's it all mean if the cosmos breaks apart and everything finally vanishes?

JENNY. That's why it's important to be held and squeezed now—by anyone willing to do the squeezing.

SHEILA. Don't try to justify screwing my husband on existential grounds.

HAL. What if you and David were also having an affair?

MAX. I thought of that, but then it starts to become silly.

JENNY. But if life is anything, it's silly.

DAVID. That's right. The philosophers call it absurd, but what they really mean is silly.

MAX. The problem is, it implies everyone is unfaithful, but it's not accurate.

HAL. But it doesn't have to be accurate if it's funny. Art is different from life.

MAX. Art is the mirror of life.

HAL. Speaking of mirrors, I always wanted to put a mirror on the ceiling over our bed, but she wouldn't go for it.

SANDY. It's the dumbest thing I ever heard.

HAL. It's sexy.

SANDY. It's adolescent. I want to make love, not watch two images of each other having intercourse from that perspective I'll just see your behind going up and down.

HAL. Why do you always ridicule my needs? Then you wonder why I sit and daydream about Holly Fox.

SANDY. Just don't tell her your mirror idea, she'll burst out laughing.

HAL. If you must know, we've done it in front of a mirror.

SANDY. In your fantasies.

HAL. In your bathroom.

SANDY. What?

DAVID. Aha! This is a juicier story than ours.

HAL. Not that I loved her or that we had an affair or anything. It was a one-shot deal.

SANDY. You and Holly Fox?

HAL. What are you acting so surprised? You've accused me of it jokingly for two years.

SANDY. I was joking.

HAL. There are no jokes. Freud said that.

SHEILA. That's my line.

SANDY. Besides, you always swore she didn't appeal to you.

HAL. That's right, I swore—I held up my right hand—I'm an agnostic.

NORMAN. Be reasonable, Sandy. No husband admits to having slept with another woman.

SANDY. He just did.

MAX. That's why my wife left me. That's why I bought your house to live alone and keep out of the rat race of romantic relationships. I was having an affair with my wife's mother.

NORMAN. My God—why isn't that in our story—it's great.

MAX. Because no one would believe it. Her father was a well-known film star—well, I don't have to tell you—he divorced her biological mother and married their au pair girl—so my wife now had a mother ten years younger than she.

JENNY. A stepmother.

MAX. It's semantics—meanwhile I was boffing her.

DAVID. So you're also cheating on your father-in-law.

MAX. That's OK because he was a shoe fetishist who could only get aroused if Prada was having a sale.

SHEILA. This does strain credulity.

MAX. My wife's mother kept a diary. Very graphic. Our intimacies—our lovemaking. Details. Names. She thought it romantic. One night my wife said to her, I'm going to the Hamptons tomorrow—I need a good book for the beach. Thinking it was her leather-bound volume of Henry James, she mistakenly gave her the leather-bound diary. I was with my wife when she read it on the beach. A change came over her—a physical change— like when the full moon comes out in a Wolfman movie.

HAL. So that's where you got the idea.

NORMAN. What'd you do?

MAX. What could I do? I denied it.

NORMAN. What'd she do?

MAX. She tried to drown herself. She ran into the ocean but only succeeded in getting stung by a jellyfish. It made her lips swell up. Suddenly with those big lips she looked sexy, and I fell back in love with her. Of course, when the swelling went down she got on my nerves again.

HAL. Well, I *wasn't* having an affair—mine was a onetime thing. At our New Year's Eve party. Everyone was downstairs drinking, partying—I happened to walk past your bathroom upstairs, Holly was in it and asked if we had any Q-tips, so I went in to help her find them, closed the door and did it with her.

DAVID. Why did she need Q-tips?

JENNY. What's the difference!?

NORMAN. Who cares about the goddamn Q-tips?

SANDY. They'd been making eyes at each other for months.

HAL. That's pure projection. You were the one with big eyes for her brother.

SANDY. If you were more perceptive you would have known I had no interest in Ken Fox.

HAL. No?

SANDY. No. If I ever would have strayed at all it would have been with Howard Nadleman.

HAL. Nadleman? The real estate agent?

SANDY. Howard Nadleman knows how to make a woman feel her sexuality.

HAL. What does that mean?

SANDY. Nothing.

HAL. You had a one-night stand with Howard Nadleman?

SANDY. No.

HAL. Thank God for that.

SANDY. We had a long romance.

HAL. You had a romance with Howard Nadleman?

SANDY. Yes, I did.

HAL. Don't deny it.

SANDY. As long as we're coming clean, I may as well be honest too.

HAL. A minute ago you said, "if I ever would have strayed at all," implying you never strayed.

SANDY. I can't live this lie anymore. With all due respect to you, I've been sleeping with Howard Nadleman.

DAVID. Go, Nadleman!

HAL. Don't make me laugh.

SANDY. I've always loved you, Hal—you know that. But what does a person do when the romance fades—when the passion drains away and you still love and respect your spouse—you cheat on him.

NORMAN. That's what I was trying to explain to Sheila.

HAL. How many times did you sleep with Howard?

SANDY. Do numbers ever really tell you anything?

HAL. Yes, I'm an accountant.

SANDY. Let's put it this way—I don't go for psychoanalysis.

HAL. You mean—all those Wednesdays, Thursdays and Saturdays—

SANDY. There is no Doctor Fineglass.

HAL. And I thought your depression was lifting.

SANDY. It was.

HAL. But a hundred and sixty dollars an hour?

SANDY. That was for the hotel rooms.

HAL. I was paying for your hotel rooms three days a week with Howard Nadleman all year?

SANDY. Didn't you notice it was strange I had the only shrink who didn't take August off?

DAVID. It turns out their life is the farce, not ours.

SHEILA. The farce, or is it tragedy?

NORMAN. Why is it tragedy?

SHEILA. It's a sorry situation—two people who must've loved one another at one time—obviously still do—but the initial excitement drains from their marriage . . .

JENNY. But no one can sustain that first rush of excitement.

DAVID. That's right—we settle in—the sexual passion is replaced by other things—shared experiences—children—beastiality.

HAL. Is it still going on with you and Nadleman?

SANDY. No—remember some months ago he suffered a brain concussion?

HAL. Yes—he's never been the same—how did it happen?

SANDY. The mirror on the ceiling over the bed fell on him.

HAL. Oh God! Him and not me!

DAVID. I'll tell you why their situation is farce—because they're pathetic. They lack tragic stature. What is he, an accountant? And she's a housewife. This is not *Hamlet* or *Medea*.

HAL. Oh please—you don't have to be a prince to suffer—there's millions of people out there every bit as tortured as Hamlet. They're Hamlet on Prozac.

SANDY. And jealous as Medea.

MAX. Therefore, what can I conclude? Everybody has their dark secrets, their longings, their lusts, their awful needs—so if life is to continue one must choose to forgive.

NORMAN. And that's where our play should go. So I took a momentary fancy to your sister—big deal—so maybe you should write it so that Sheila and David once spent a passionate night together—so we all learn each other's pathetic shortcomings and we forgive each other.

JENNY. Yes. And the audience laughs at all of us and they escape from their own sad lives for a brief moment and then we kiss and make up.

MAX. Forgiveness—it gives this little sex farce dimension and heart.

SHEILA. That's right. Who am I to judge others and throw away years of closeness and love because my husband the dentist was drilling my sister?

JENNY. We'll change—we'll make amends. Where there's life there's hope.

SANDY. But how is forgiveness different than just sweeping all your problems under the rug?

MAX. It's much grander—it takes a bigger person—forgiveness is divine.

JENNY. And maybe it's the same but it sounds better.

MAX. I like it—it's funny, it's sad, and best of all, it's commercial. Come—let's go to my study so I can complete the third act while it's all fresh—I feel my writer's block lifting. The key word is "commercial"—I'm sorry, "forgiveness"—the key word is "forgiveness."

(They go upstairs together. The MAXWELLS look at each other.)

HAL. I don't think I can forgive you, Sandy.

SANDY. No. Nor I, you.

HAL. I don't know why. I know Max Krolian is right—he's a deep playwright.

SANDY. It's easy to forgive in fiction—the author can manipulate reality. And as you say, Krolian's a clever craftsman.

HAL. I can't believe you had a long affair with Howard Nadleman—he was probably getting even with me for the audit.

SANDY. It had nothing to do with you—everything is not always about you.

HAL. Was I such an unromantic husband?

SANDY. As the years went by you stopped trying.

HAL. I became discouraged. You started taking me for granted too.

SANDY. All those imaginary characters can be rewritten—their lives erased, begun again—but we've said and done things that can never be erased.

HAL. The tragic part is that I love you.

SANDY. And I love you, but it's pathetic, not tragic.

HAL. If I took that rifle and killed us both I could redeem our infidelities with one grand gesture.

SANDY. You're not the type, Hal. Accountants don't commit suicide and find redemption—they usually just vanish and turn up in the Cayman islands.

HAL. What do you want to do?

SANDY. What can we do? Sweep the painful aspects of the relationship under the rug and call it forgiveness or get a divorce.

HAL. Sandy—this was the first room we made love in. Can't we start over?

SANDY. Clean starts work better in fiction.

HAL. But every life needs a little fiction in it—too much reality is a very nasty thing.

SANDY. Maybe now that everything's out in the open . . . What's that honking sound?

HAL. *(To window.)* Look at all those geese.

SANDY. *(Joining him.)* My goodness—we never had geese when we lived here.

HAL. It's a symbol.

SANDY. Of what?

HAL. Of a fresh start—of geese where geese never were. Today was a day full of symbols—full of writing, of characters, of literature. The poet that beats 'neath the breast of this accountant came out and I helped Max Krolian write a warm ending to his play—only you and I remained unresolved, undecided and confused—we were looking for some sign—some way to recapture the music in our relationship and then—the honking of the geese—

SANDY. And you see it as a symbol.

HAL. Don't you see, Sandy? Can't you see what they're trying to tell us? Don't you know one simple fact about geese? Geese mate forever.

SANDY. Do geese have affairs?

HAL. If they do they work it out somehow—it's all in nature's design.

SANDY. Could it really be my husband is a poet trapped in the body of a CPA?

(Sound of geese honking, and music rises. Kiss.)

FADE OUT

OTHER TITLES AVAILABLE FROM SAMUEL FRENCH

GETTING AND SPENDING
Michael J. Chepiga

Dramatic Comedy / 4m, 3f
A brilliant and beautiful investment banker makes illegal profits of eighteen million dollars from insider trading and uses it to build housing for the homeless. Shortly before her trial, she ferrets out the foremost criminal attorney of the era to persuade him to abandon his retirement in a Kentucky monastery to defend her. This play is about them: their struggles with themselves, with each other, with the law and with her unusual defense.

"Stirs the conscience while entertaining the spirit."
– *Los Angeles Times*

"An off beat, audacious comedy, well worth seeing."
– *WNBC TV*

THE DOWNSIDE
Richard Dresser

Comedy / 6m, 2f / Combined Interior
American business is the target of this hilarious and cutting satire originally produced at Long Wharf Theatre. A pharmaceutical firm has acquired rights to market a European anti stress drug and marketing has got to come up with a snazzy ad campaign. Nowhere is this drug more needed than right here at Mark & Maxwell to counter corporate ineptitude. The strategy meetings get more pointless and frenetic as the deadline approaches. These meetings are chaired by Dave who is never actually there; he is a voice directing the campaign from his mobile phone while jetting between meetings, unstoppable even when his plane is hijacked.

"Funny and ruthlessly cynical."
– *Philadelphia Inquirer*

"Sheer delight."
– *Westport News*

MUSIC FROM DOWN THE HILL
John Ford Noonan

Drama / 2f / Interior

The setting is a psychiatric clinic atop a hill in the beautiful country town of Woodstock, New York. Claire Granick, a young schizophrenic who loves Bruce Springsteen to death and cannot for the life of her tell the truth, regularly drives out new roommates with terror tactics and Springsteen songs played too loud. Enter Margot Yossarian, a middle aged hysteric with a huge heart and a frightened body who also loves rock n roll, especially the music of the 60s: Hendrix, Joplin, The Doors, Cream. Claire's usually effective tactics don't undermine Margot, but rather release her stiffened body and send her to a soaring state of health dreamed of but never expected by the head of the hospital. In Act II, Margot attempts to help Claire break through her problems. Is she successful? Is rock n roll truly deep and loud enough to heal the mentally disturbed? Can the concept of rock penetrate the disturbed heart and create a miracle of mental health? Do people this disturbed ever successfully get back to the outside?

"A delicacy of feeling that is rare in theatre pieces today.... A cannily constructed melange of alienation [and] nostalgia..."
– *The New York Times*

SAMUEL FRENCH STAFF

Nate Collins
President

Ken Dingledine
Director of Operations,
Vice President

Bruce Lazarus
Executive Director,
General Counsel

Rita Maté
Director of Finance

ACCOUNTING

Lori Thimsen | Director of Licensing Compliance
Nehal Kumar | Senior Accounting Associate
Josephine Messina | Accounts Payable
Helena Mezzina | Royalty Administration
Joe Garner | Royalty Administration
Jessica Zheng | Accounts Receivable
Andy Lian | Accounts Receivable
Zoe Qiu | Accounts Receivable
Charlie Sou | Accounting Associate
Joann Mannello | Orders Administrator

BUSINESS AFFAIRS

Lysna Marzani | Director of Business Affairs
Kathryn McCumber | Business Administrator

CUSTOMER SERVICE AND LICENSING

Brad Lohrenz | Director of Licensing Development
Fred Schnitzer | Business Development Manager
Laura Lindson | Licensing Services Manager
Kim Rogers | Professional Licensing Associate
Matthew Akers | Amateur Licensing Associate
Ashley Byrne | Amateur Licensing Associate
Glenn Halcomb | Amateur Licensing Associate
Derek Hassler | Amateur Licensing Associate
Jennifer Carter | Amateur Licensing Associate
Kelly McCready | Amateur Licensing Associate
Annette Storckman | Amateur Licensing Associate
Chris Lonstrup | Outgoing Information Specialist

EDITORIAL AND PUBLICATIONS

Amy Rose Marsh | Literary Manager
Ben Coleman | Editorial Associate
Gene Sweeney | Graphic Designer
David Geer | Publications Supervisor
Charlyn Brea | Publications Associate
Tyler Mullen | Publications Associate

MARKETING

Abbie Van Nostrand | Director of Corporate
Communications
Ryan Pointer | Marketing Manager
Courtney Kochuba | Marketing Associate

OPERATIONS

Joe Ferreira | Product Development Manager
Casey McLain | Operations Supervisor
Danielle Heckman | Office Coordinator, Reception

SAMUEL FRENCH BOOKSHOP (LOS ANGELES)

Joyce Mehess | Bookstore Manager
Cory DeLair | Bookstore Buyer
Jennifer Palumbo | Customer Service Associate
Sonya Wallace | Bookstore Associate
Tim Coultas | Bookstore Associate
Monté Patterson | Bookstore Associate
Robin Hushbeck | Bookstore Associate
Alfred Contreras | Shipping & Receiving

LONDON OFFICE

Felicity Barks | Rights & Contracts Associate
Steve Blacker | Bookshop Associate
David Bray | Customer Services Associate
Zena Choi | Professional Licensing Associate
Robert Cooke | Assistant Buyer
Stephanie Dawson | Amateur Licensing Associate
Simon Ellison | Retail Sales Manager
Jason Felix | Royalty Administration
Susan Griffiths | Amateur Licensing Associate
Robert Hamilton | Amateur Licensing Associate
Lucy Hume | Publications Manager
Nasir Khan | Management Accountant
Simon Magniti | Royalty Administration
Louise Mappley | Amateur Licensing Associate
James Nicolau | Despatch Associate
Martin Phillips | Librarian
Zubayed Rahman | Despatch Associate
Steve Sanderson | Royalty Administration Supervisor
Douglas Schatz | Acting Executive Director
Roger Sheppard | I.T. Manager
Geoffrey Skinner | Company Accountant
Peter Smith | Amateur Licensing Associate
Garry Spratley | Customer Service Manager
David Webster | UK Operations Director